HOW TO DRAW PLANES

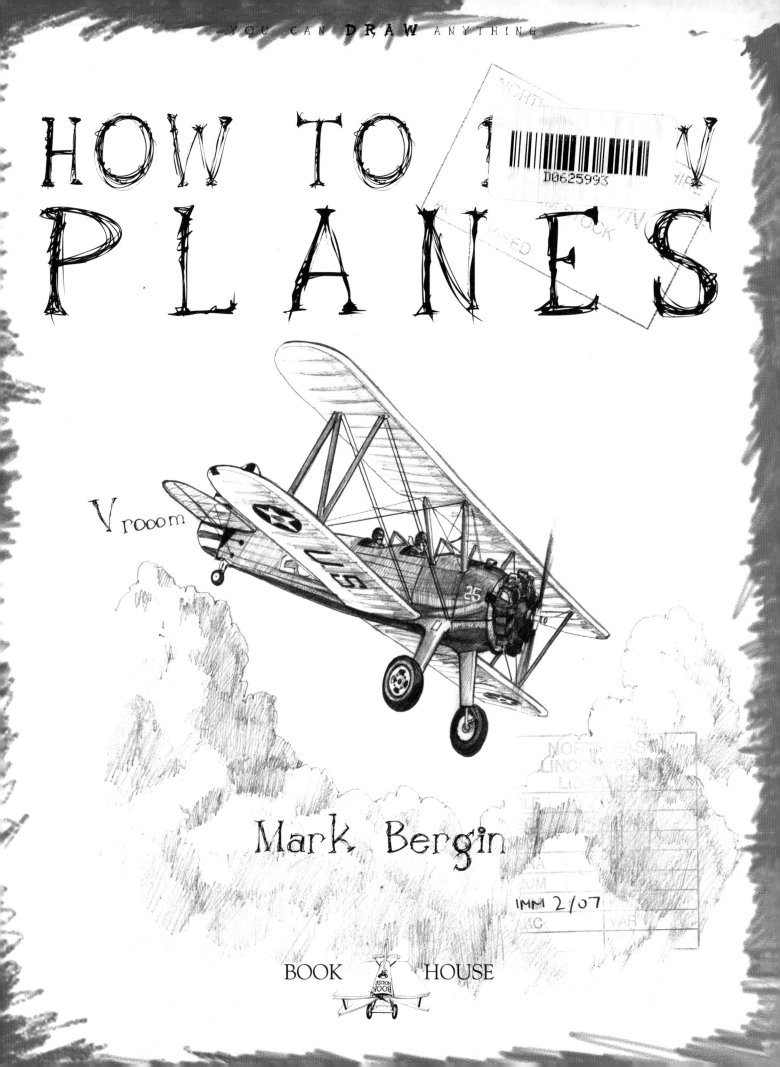

Vrooom

Mark Bergin

BOOK HOUSE

Published in Great Britain in 2006 by
Book House, an imprint of
The Salariya Book Company Ltd
25 Marlborough Place, Brighton, BN1 1UB

SALARIYA

North East Lincolnshire Council	
Askews	
	£4.99

Please visit The Salariya Book Company at: **www.salariya.com**

Author: Mark Bergin was born in Hastings in 1961. He studied
at Eastbourne College of Art and has specialised in historical
reconstructions, aviation and maritime subjects since 1983. He
lives in Bexhill-on-Sea with his wife and three children.

Editor: Sophie Izod
Editorial Assistant: Mark Williams

PB ISBN-10: 1-904642-70-5
PB ISBN-13: 978-1-904642-70-1

A CIP catalogue record for this book is
available from the British Library.

Printed and bound in China.
Printed on paper from sustainable sources.

*Fixatives should be used under
adult supervision.

Contents

Making a start

Learning to draw is about looking and seeing. Keep practicing and get to know your subject. Use a sketchbook to make quick sketches. Start by doodling, and experiment with shapes and patterns. There are many ways to draw, this book shows one method. Visit art galleries, look at artists' drawings, see how friends draw, and most importantly, find your own way.

Supermarine Spitfire

Remember that it is practice that will make the drawing work, if it looks wrong, start again. Keep working at it — the more you draw, the more you will learn.

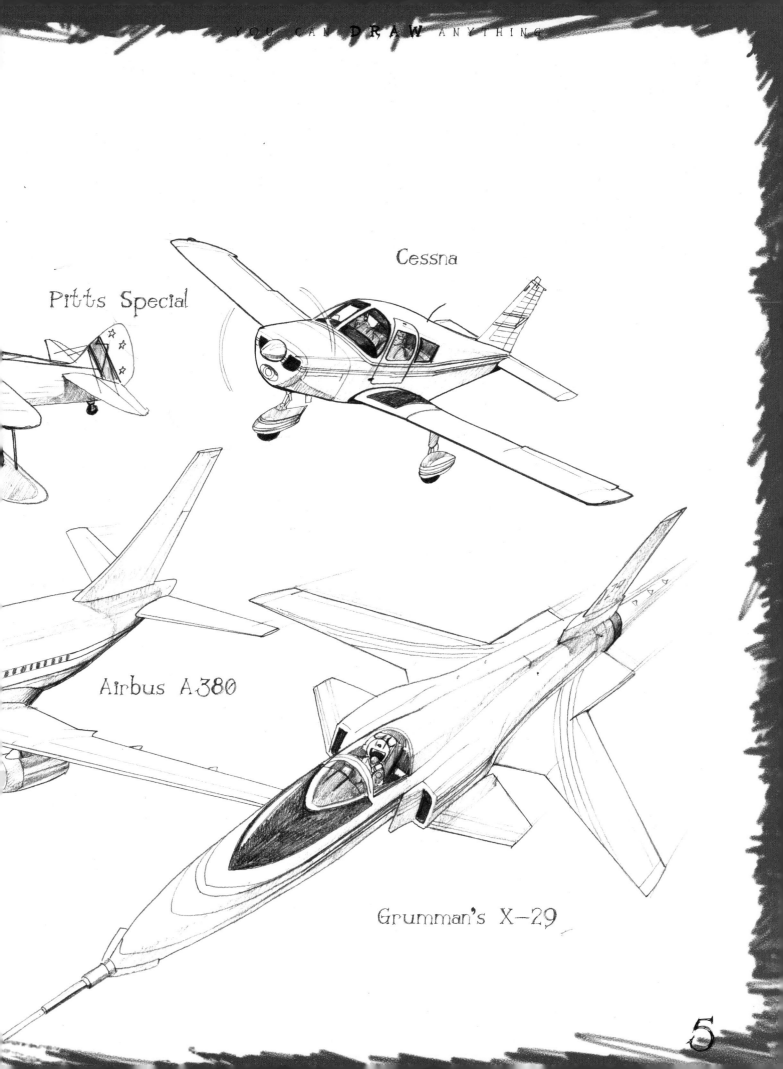

Cessna

Pitts Special

Airbus A380

Grumman's X-29

Perspective

If you look at a plane from different viewpoints, you will see that the part of the plane that is closest to you will look larger, and the part furthest away from you will look smaller. Drawing in perspective is a way of creating a feeling of space and three— dimensions on a flat surface.

(Below) Note how the circular construction lines are larger the nearer they are to your viewpoint. The circles are smaller at the rear of the plane, because that is furthest away from your viewpoint.

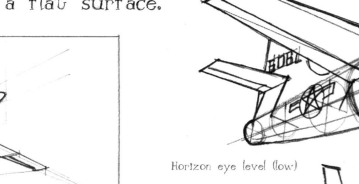

Horizon eye level (low)

Horizon eye level (low)

V.P   V.P

Horizon eye level

Horizon

V.P.   V.P

Horizon eye level (high)

V.P   V.P

Horizon eye level (high)

(Above) Note how the circular construction lines are larger the nearer they are to the centre of the plane.

6

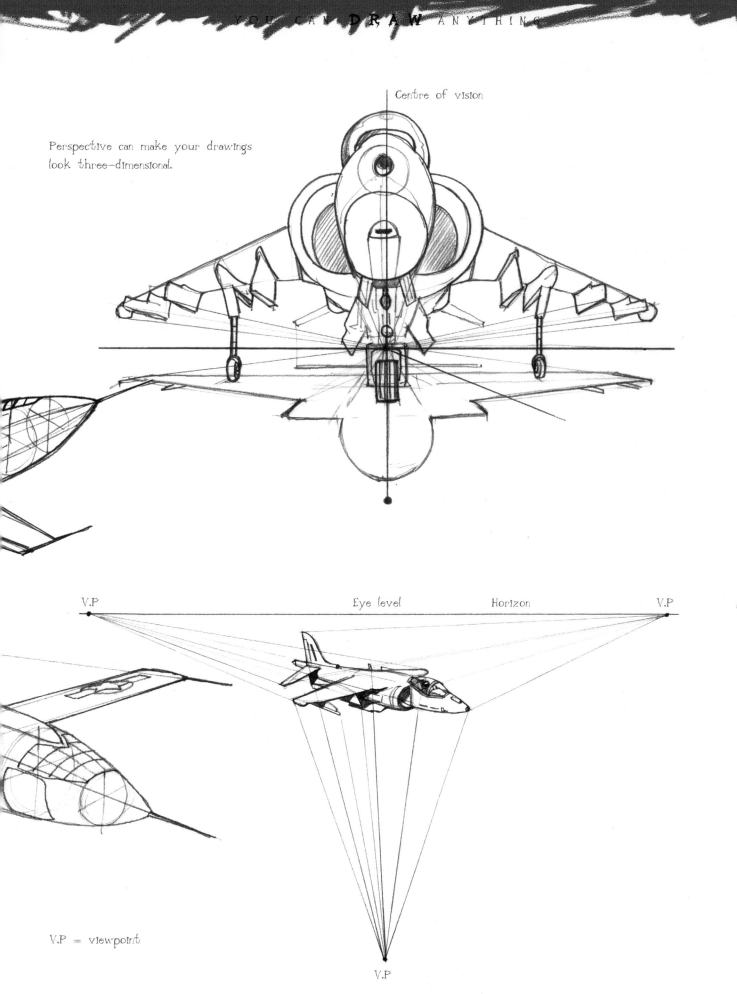

Centre of vision

Perspective can make your drawings
look three-dimensional.

V.P   Eye level   Horizon   V.P

V.P = viewpoint

V.P

Using photographs

It is important that you consider the position of your drawing on the paper, this is called composition. Drawing from a photograph can help you identify shape and form.

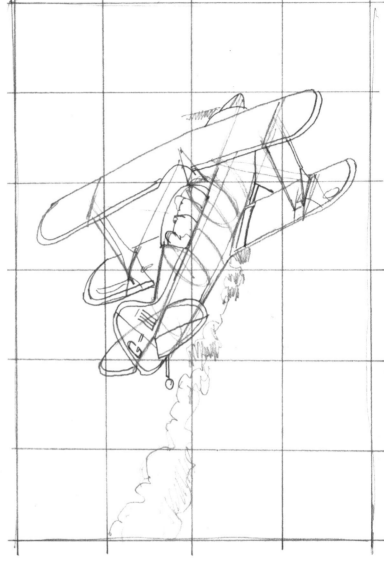

(Below) Make a tracing of the photograph and draw a grid over it.

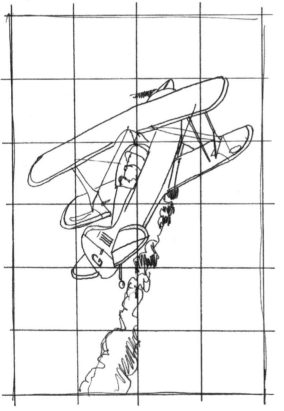

(Above) Then draw another grid, enlarging or reducing it to the same scale. You can now transfer the outline shapes from your tracing, to the paper, using your grid as a guide.

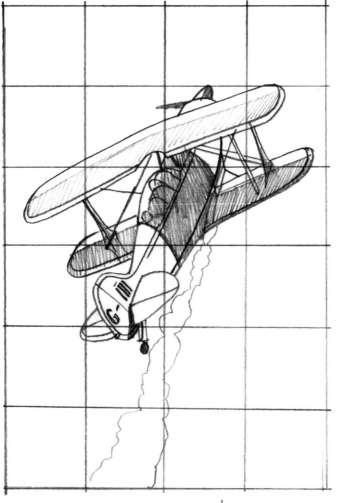

(Left) You must remember that the photograph is flat. You need to make your drawing look three-dimensional. See how light falls on the plane.

(Above) Use construction lines to help you work out the three-dimensional shape.

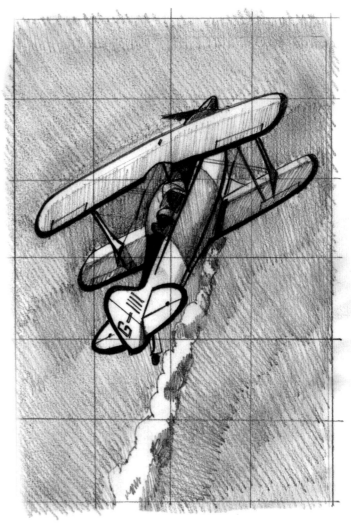

Materials

Try using different drawing papers and materials. Experiment with charcoal, wax crayons, and pastels. Pens, from felt-tips to ball-points will all make interesting marks, or try drawing with pen and ink on wet paper.

Pencil

Remember, the best equipment and materials will not necessarily make the best drawing.

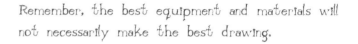

Felt-tip pen

MX

Pencils are graded from 6H (the hardest) through 5H, 4H, 3H, 2H to H, then B through 1B, 2B, 3B, 4B, 5B up to 6B (the softest).

Charcoal is very soft and can be used for big, bold drawings. Spray charcoal with fixative* to prevent further smudging (see page 2).

Pastels are even softer than charcoal, and come in a wide range of colours. Spray pastels with fixative* to prevent further smudging (see page 2).

Special effects can be achieved by scraping away parts of a drawing done with wax **crayons**.

Lines drawn in ink cannot be erased, so drawings can look more free, and mistakes can be lost in the drawing.

Line pens

Ink

Sketching

We can't always rely on our memories, so we have to look around and find real—life things we want to draw. Using a sketchbook is one of the best ways to build drawing skills. Learn to observe objects: see how they move, how they are made and how they work. What you draw should be what you have seen. Since the Renaissance, artists have used sketchbooks to record their ideas and drawings.

Sketching

A sketch that has taken a short time can say as much as a careful drawing that has taken many hours.

Sketching models

Try drawing model planes. It will be good practice for seeing and observing. The larger the model is, the better it is to draw because its proportions are better.

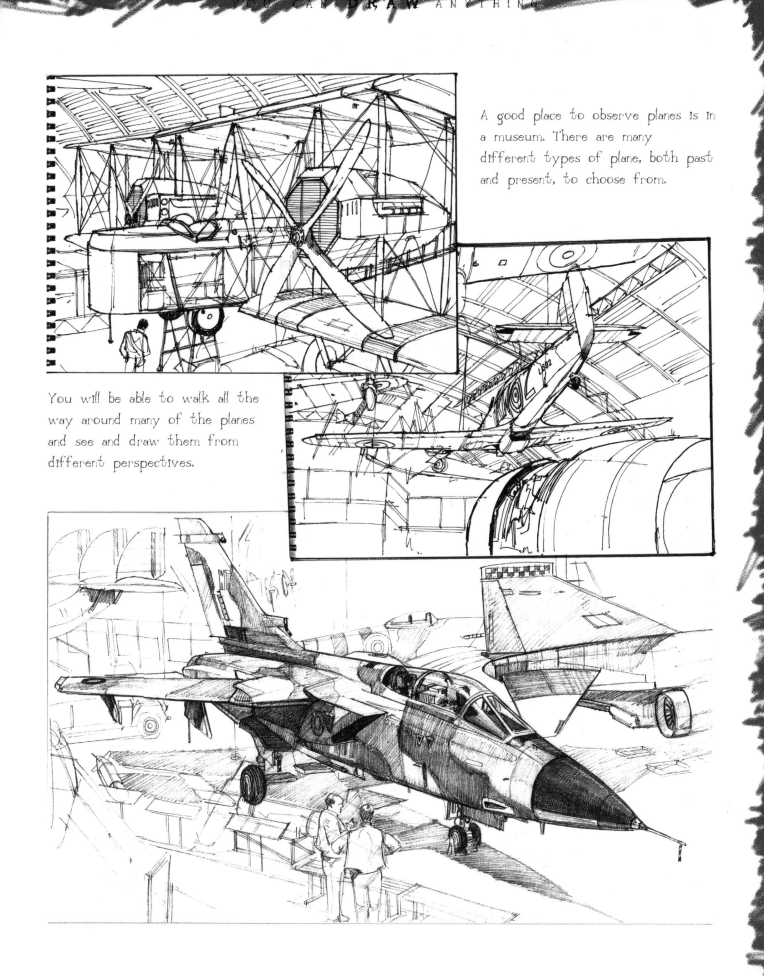

A good place to observe planes is in a museum. There are many different types of plane, both past and present, to choose from.

You will be able to walk all the way around many of the planes and see and draw them from different perspectives.

Fokker DR1 Triplane

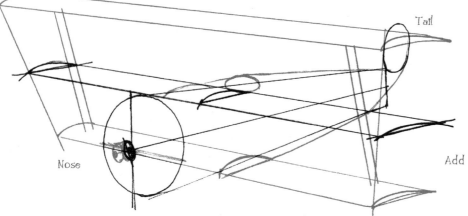

The Fokker Dreidecker (DR1) triplane was used by Germany in WW1 against the British Sopwith triplane. It carried one pilot and was armed with two machine guns. Its most famous pilot was Baron Manfred von Richthofen.

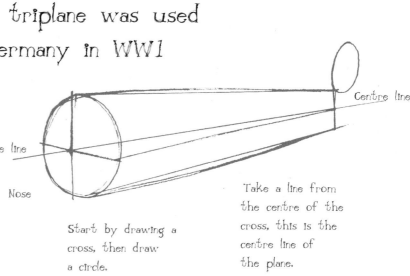

Centre line

Centre line

Nose

Start by drawing a cross, then draw a circle.

Take a line from the centre of the cross, this is the centre line of the plane.

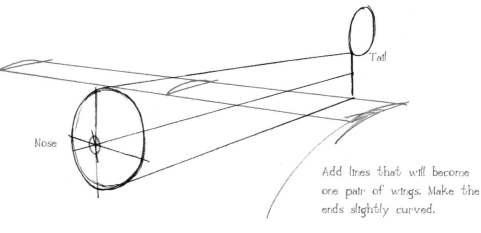

Tail

Nose

Add lines that will become one pair of wings. Make the ends slightly curved.

Tail

Now add lines that will become the other wings.

Nose

Add supports for the wings.

The DR1 was a difficult aircraft to fly, and was regarded as a machine strictly for experienced pilots.

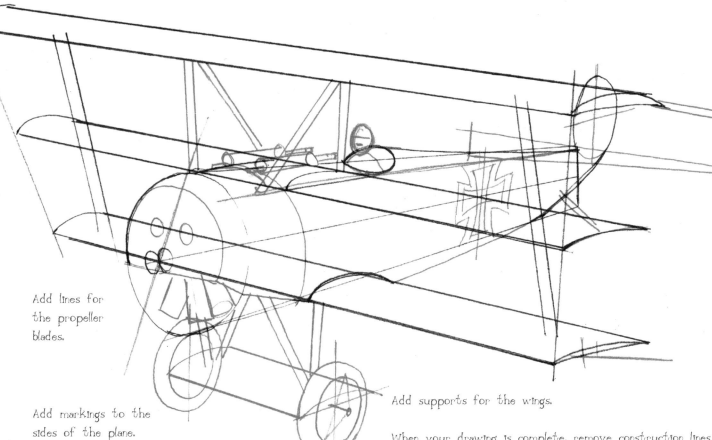

Add lines for the propeller blades.

Add markings to the sides of the plane.

Add supports for the wings.

When your drawing is complete, remove construction lines with an eraser.

Backgrounds
Try adding a background to your picture.

Baron Manfred von Richthofen was born in Breslau, Germany (now Wroclaw, Poland) and died on 21 April 1918, aged 25, in the skies over Vaux sur Somme, France. The Germans called him *Der Rote Kampfflieger* ("The Red Battle-Flyer"), the French called him *le petit rouge* ("the little red") and in Britain he was known as the Red Baron.

Supermarine Spitfire

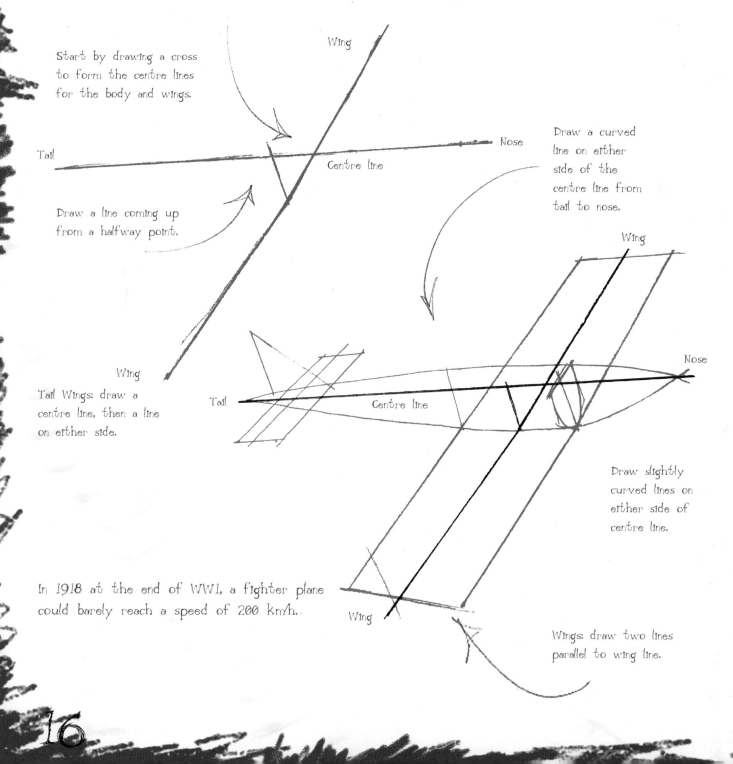

In the summer of 1940, fewer than a thousand British Hurricanes and Supermarine Spitfire planes defeated 3,000 aircraft in the *Luftwaffe* (German airforce).

Start by drawing a cross to form the centre lines for the body and wings.

Wing

Tail

Centre line

Nose

Draw a line coming up from a halfway point.

Draw a curved line on either side of the centre line from tail to nose.

Wing

Wing

Tail Wings: draw a centre line, then a line on either side.

Tail

Centre line

Nose

Draw slightly curved lines on either side of centre line.

In 1918 at the end of WW1, a fighter plane could barely reach a speed of 200 km/h.

Wing

Wings: draw two lines parallel to wing line.

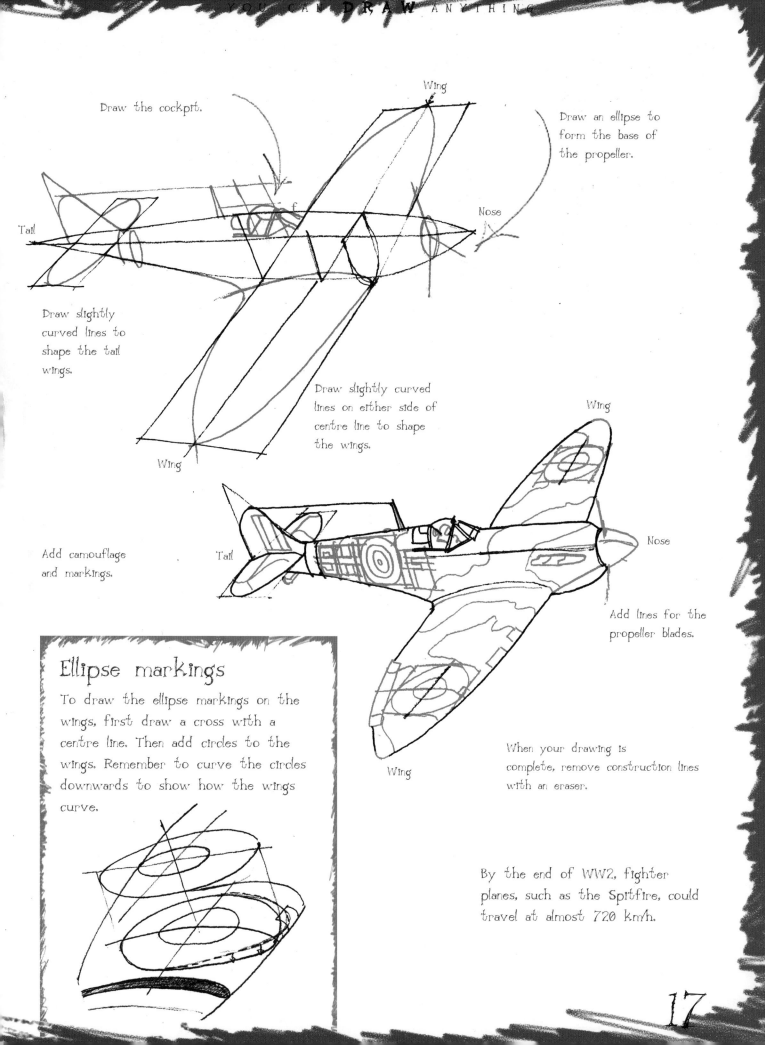

Draw the cockpit.

Wing

Draw an ellipse to form the base of the propeller.

Tail

Nose

Draw slightly curved lines to shape the tail wings.

Draw slightly curved lines on either side of centre line to shape the wings.

Wing

Wing

Add camouflage and markings.

Tail

Nose

Add lines for the propeller blades.

Ellipse markings

To draw the ellipse markings on the wings, first draw a cross with a centre line. Then add circles to the wings. Remember to curve the circles downwards to show how the wings curve.

Wing

When your drawing is complete, remove construction lines with an eraser.

By the end of WW2, fighter planes, such as the Spitfire, could travel at almost 720 km/h.

17

Supermarine S6B

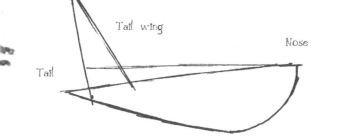

The Supermarine S6B Seaplane became the fastest aircraft on Earth in September 1931 when it achieved a record—breaking speed of 656 km/h.

Tail wing

Tail

Nose

Start with a triangular shape with one curved side.

Tail wing

Tail

Nose

Draw two triangles, these will become part of the landing gear.

Tail

Add rectangles to the triangles.

The Supermarine S6B won the Schneider Trophy Seaplane contests for speed over a set course, for the third successive year — and outright — on 12 September 1931.

Light and dark

Shading can make your drawing appear three-dimensional.

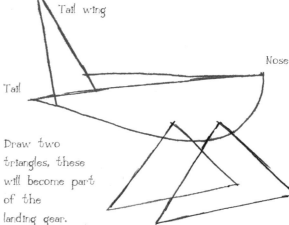

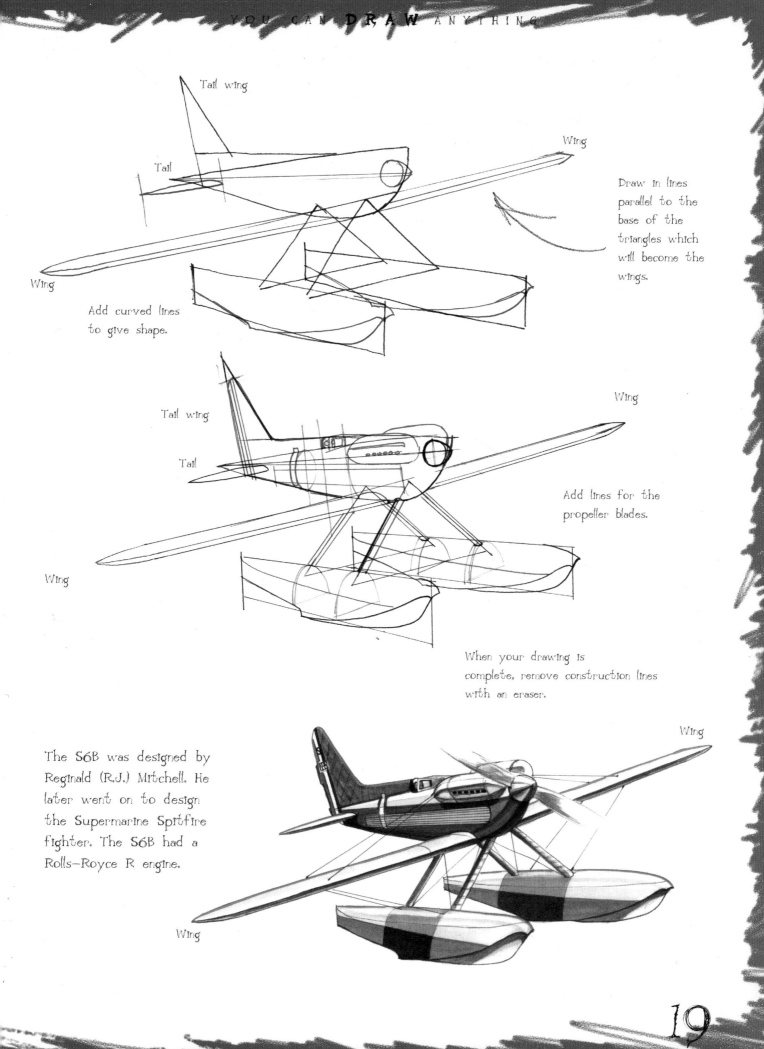

Tail wing

Tail

Wing

Wing

Draw in lines parallel to the base of the triangles which will become the wings.

Add curved lines to give shape.

Tail wing

Tail

Wing

Wing

Add lines for the propeller blades.

When your drawing is complete, remove construction lines with an eraser.

Wing

The S6B was designed by Reginald (R.J.) Mitchell. He later went on to design the Supermarine Spitfire fighter. The S6B had a Rolls-Royce R engine.

Wing

19

Pitts Special

One of the world's most famous stunt planes, the Pitts Special, was designed in 1944 in Florida, by Curtis Pitts.

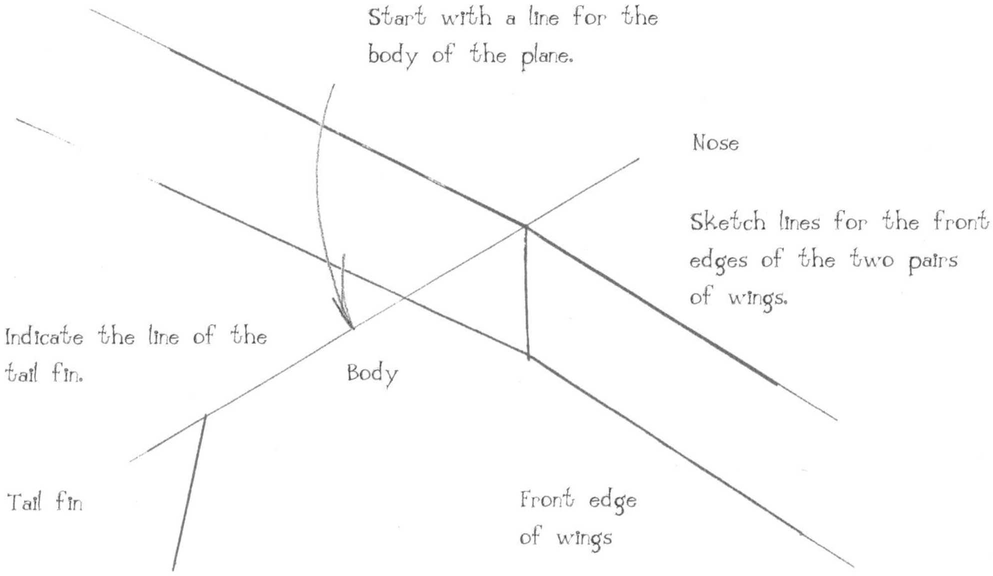

Start with a line for the body of the plane.

Nose

Sketch lines for the front edges of the two pairs of wings.

Indicate the line of the tail fin.

Body

Tail fin

Front edge of wings

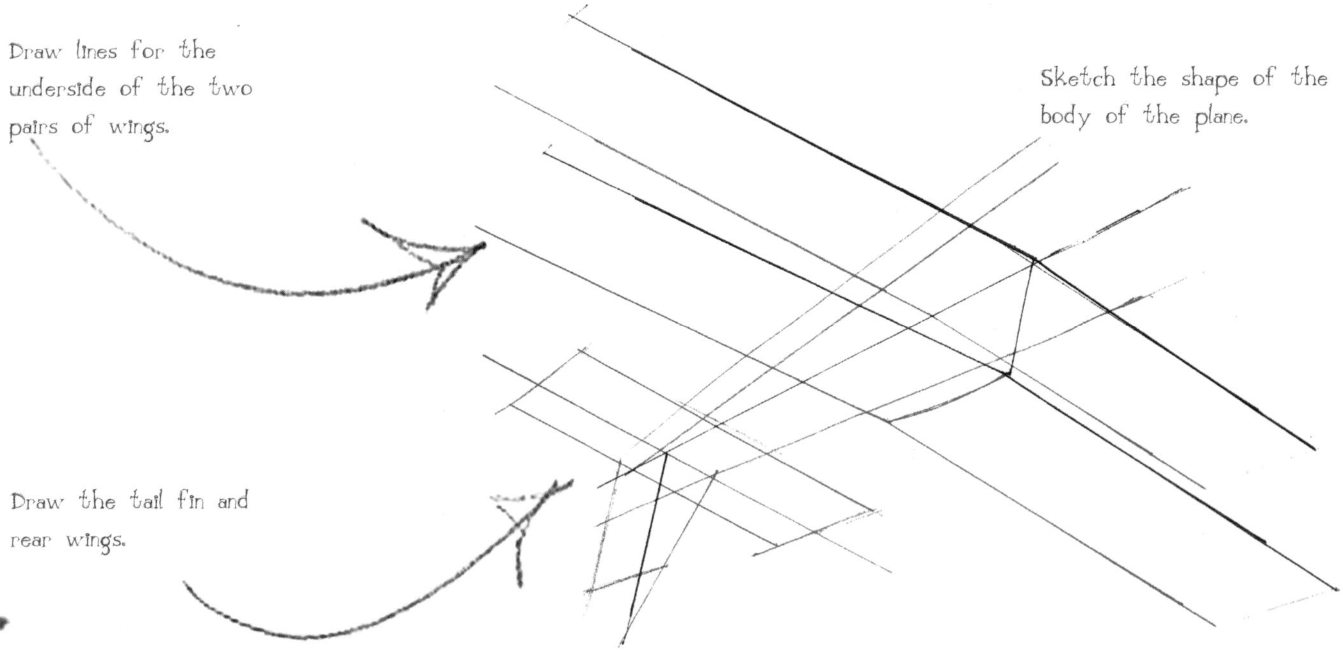

Draw lines for the underside of the two pairs of wings.

Sketch the shape of the body of the plane.

Draw the tail fin and rear wings.

Continuing to compete until the early 1980s, the Pitts Special won more aerobatic contests than any other type of aircraft.

Reverse

You can often see why a drawing is not working by looking at it in a mirror.

Put in the struts that join the two pairs of wings.

Sketch in the landing gear and wheels.

Draw the nose cone and indicate the propeller blades. Finish drawing the rounded shape of the plane's nose.

Aerofoil

Tail fin

Draw the cockpit, and loosely sketch in the pilot.

Draw the four curved wing tips and the rectangular aerofoils.

Aerofoil

Sketch the curved shape of the tail wings and fin.

When your drawing is complete, remove construction lines with an eraser.

21

'Blackbird'

The Lockheed SR-71, or 'Blackbird', is the world's fastest jet plane. It reached a speed of 3,529 km/h, over three times the speed of sound, in 1976. The SR-71 was used for spying.

Draw a line for the rear of the plane's wing.

Tail

Draw a line on either side of the line of the body.

Body

Draw a longer line from the rear of the plane to its nose.

Nose

Draw two triangular shapes to indicate the tails on the engines.

Engine tail

Tail

Engine tail

Draw a large triangle to form the wings.

Draw two curved lines to make the front of the aircraft.

Sketch a rectangle from the nose of the plane to the rear. Make the shape slightly wider at the front.

Nose

22

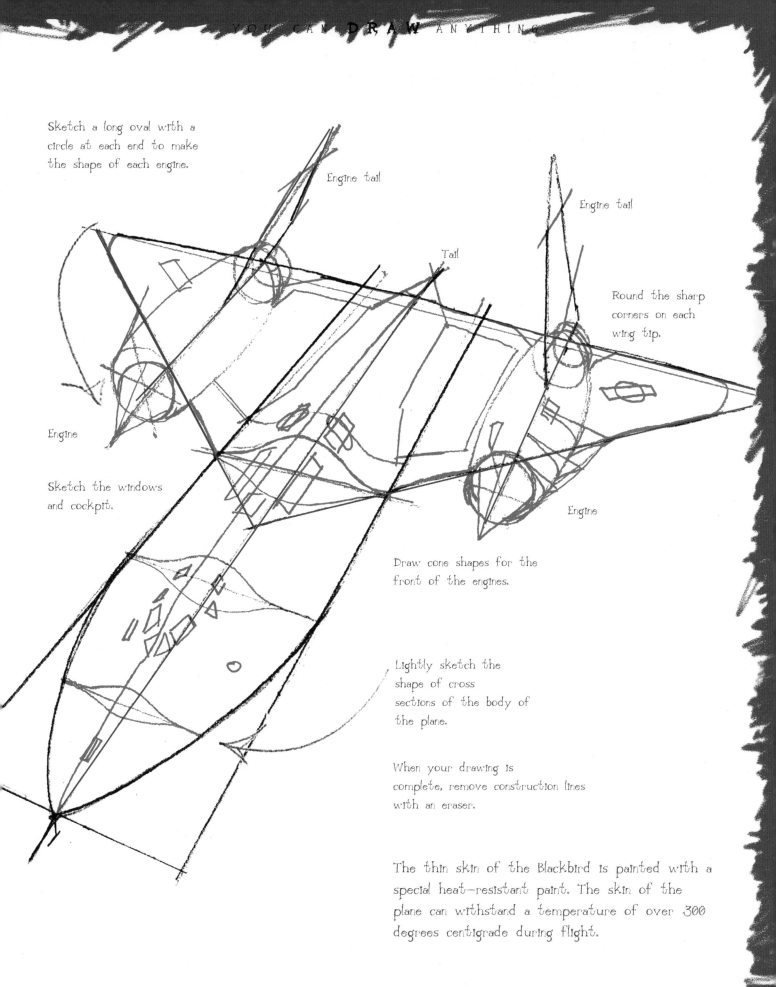

Sketch a long oval with a circle at each end to make the shape of each engine.

Engine tail

Engine tail

Tail

Round the sharp corners on each wing tip.

Engine

Sketch the windows and cockpit.

Engine

Draw cone shapes for the front of the engines.

Lightly sketch the shape of cross sections of the body of the plane.

When your drawing is complete, remove construction lines with an eraser.

The thin skin of the Blackbird is painted with a special heat-resistant paint. The skin of the plane can withstand a temperature of over 300 degrees centigrade during flight.

Concorde

oncorde had four specially designed Rolls–Royce engines. These provided the extra power needed for take off and the transition to supersonic flight. It was the most powerful pure jet–engine flying commercially.

Draw a line from the nose of the Concorde to its rear.

Rear

Wings

Lightly sketch a large triangle to form the wings.

Nose

Draw the position of the tail fin.

Sketch in the body and the long pointed nose of Concorde.

Nose

Composition
Make a cardboard frame and use it on your drawing to find the best composition.

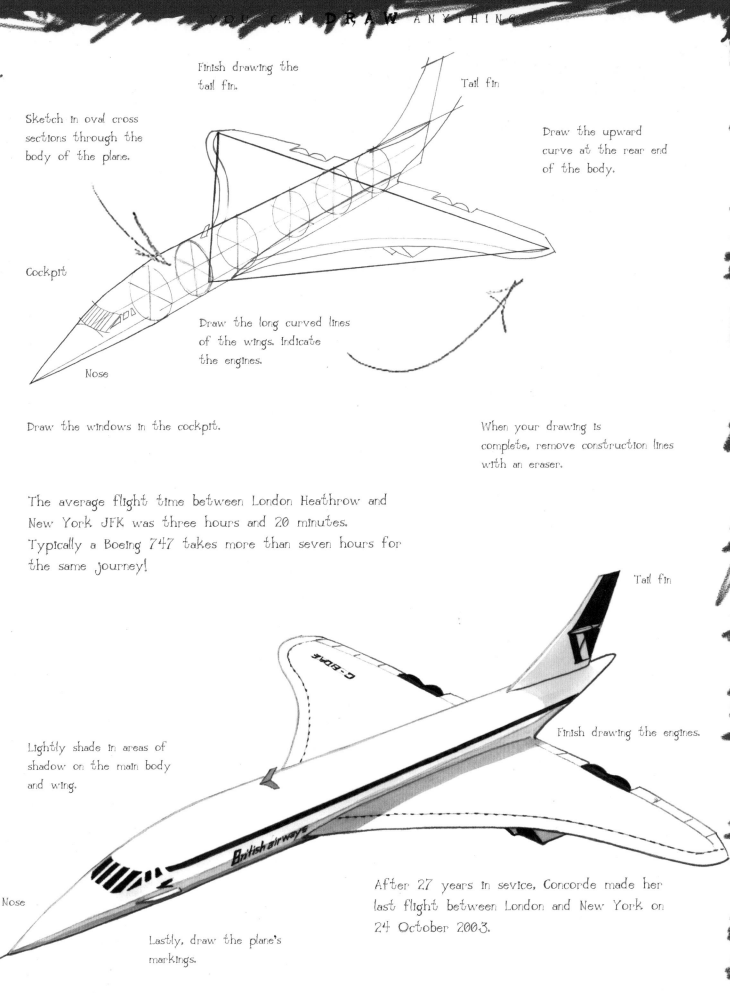

Finish drawing the
tail fin.

Tail fin

Sketch in oval cross
sections through the
body of the plane.

Draw the upward
curve at the rear end
of the body.

Cockpit

Nose

Draw the long curved lines
of the wings. Indicate
the engines.

Draw the windows in the cockpit.

When your drawing is
complete, remove construction lines
with an eraser.

The average flight time between London Heathrow and
New York JFK was three hours and 20 minutes.
Typically a Boeing 747 takes more than seven hours for
the same journey!

Tail fin

Finish drawing the engines.

Lightly shade in areas of
shadow on the main body
and wing.

Nose

Lastly, draw the plane's
markings.

After 27 years in sevice, Concorde made her
last flight between London and New York on
24 October 2003.

25

F-16A Fighting Falcon

The F-16A Fighting Falcon is a compact and manoeuvrable fighter aircraft. It is highly effective in both air-to-air combat and air-to-surface attacks.

Draw a line from the nose of the plane to its rear.

Nose

Draw a line to indicate the rear of the wings.

Rear of wings

Indicate the angle of the rear tail fin.

Rear

Sketch in the pointed shape of the nose.

Draw a long cylinder for the Falcon's body.

Nose

Sketch the Falcon's rear wings and tail fins.

Draw the front edges of the wings and indicate the wing tips.

Draw a blunt cone shape at the rear of the body.

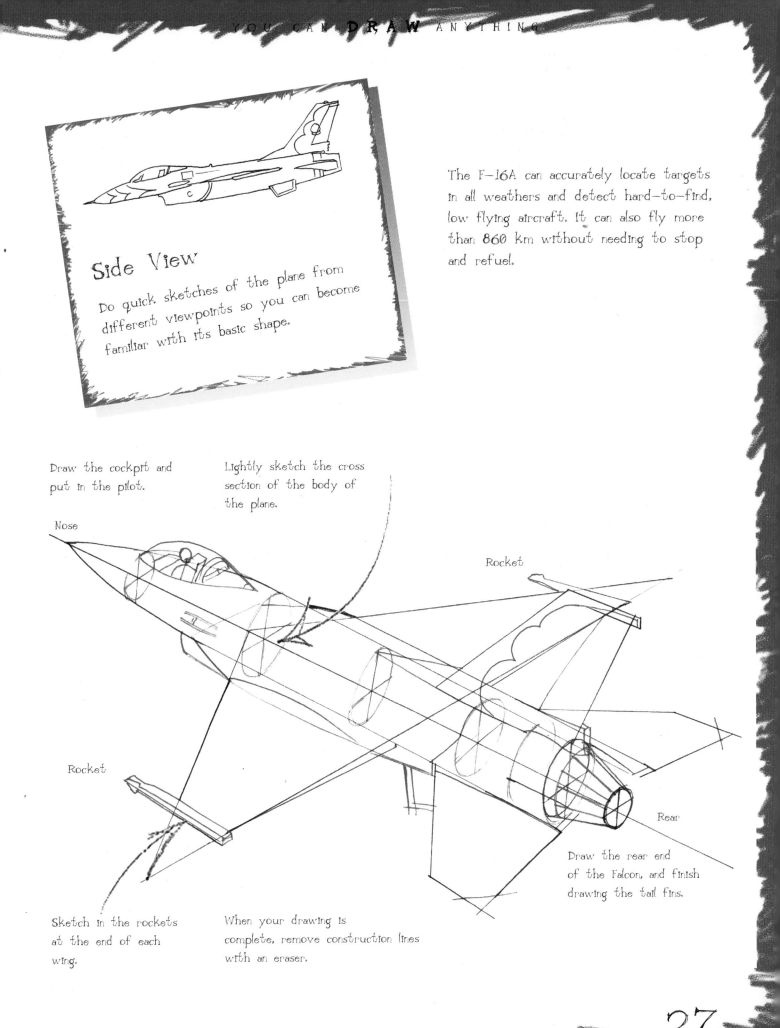

Side View

Do quick sketches of the plane from different viewpoints so you can become familiar with its basic shape.

The F–16A can accurately locate targets in all weathers and detect hard–to–find, low flying aircraft. It can also fly more than 860 km without needing to stop and refuel.

Draw the cockpit and put in the pilot.

Lightly sketch the cross section of the body of the plane.

Nose

Rocket

Rocket

Rear

Draw the rear end of the Falcon, and finish drawing the tail fins.

Sketch in the rockets at the end of each wing.

When your drawing is complete, remove construction lines with an eraser.

27

Airbus A380

T he 555 seat, double-decker Airbus A380 will be the world's largest passenger carrying airliner.

Draw the back pair of wings.

Draw a line from the rear of the plane to its nose.

Tail

Nose

Draw the front pair of wings.

Several variations of A380 planes are planned, the basic aircraft is the 555 seat A380-800. It can fly 15,000 km without refuelling.

Indicate the angle of the rear tail fin.

Tail

Ellipse

Ellipse

Ellipse

Draw in three ellipses, then join them together to form the body of the plane.

Nose

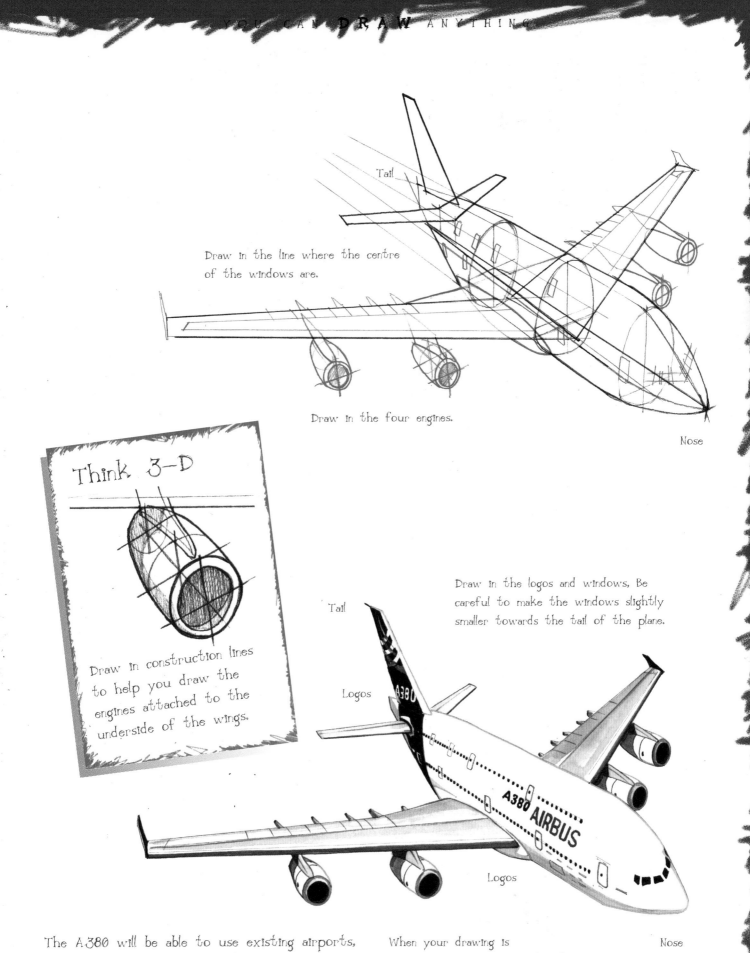

Draw in the line where the centre of the windows are.

Tail

Draw in the four engines.

Nose

Think 3-D

Draw in construction lines to help you draw the engines attached to the underside of the wings.

Tail

Logos

Draw in the logos and windows, Be careful to make the windows slightly smaller towards the tail of the plane.

A380

A380 AIRBUS

Logos

Nose

The A380 will be able to use existing airports, they have also been designed to create lower fuel emissions and less noise.

When your drawing is complete, remove construction lines with an eraser.

Space Ship One

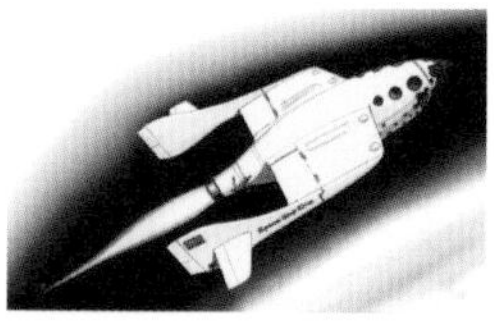

Space Ship One made the first privately-funded space flight on 21 June 2004. It is hoped that this is the future of space tourism. Thousands of people are expected to leave the Earth's atmosphere each year.

First, draw two lines that cross over.

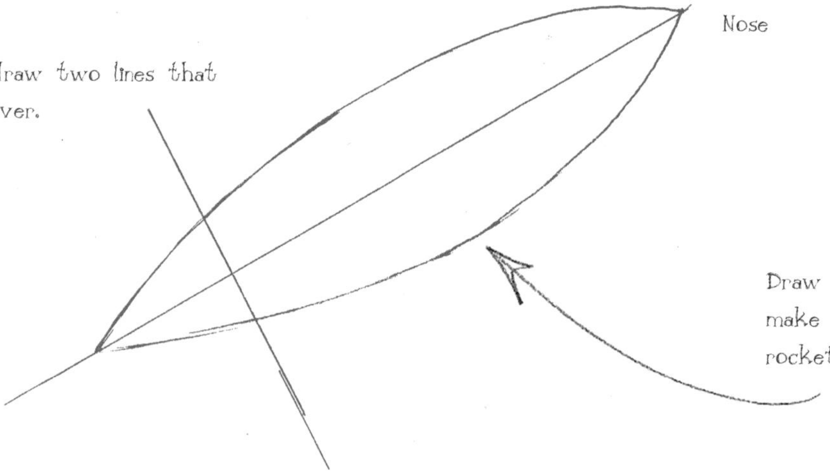

Nose

Draw two curved lines to make the sides of the rocket.

Tail

Draw a square in perspective, to form the basis of the wings.

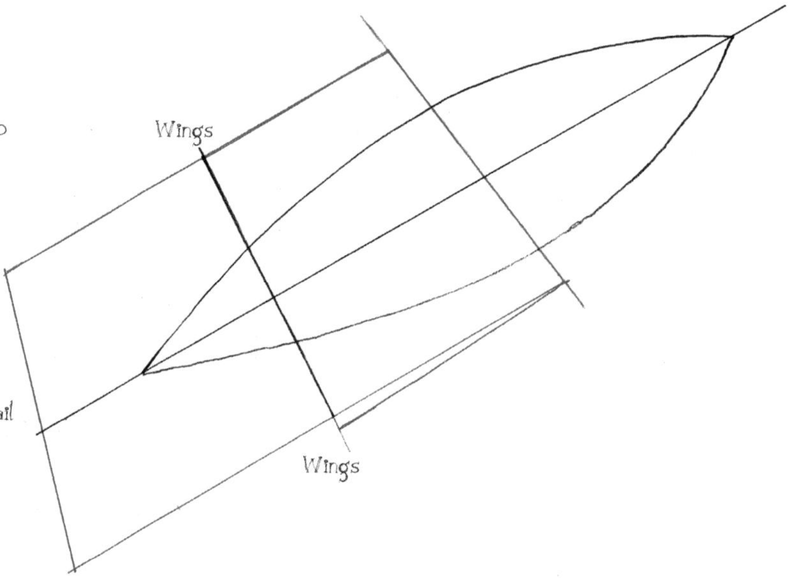

Wings

Nose

Tail

Wings

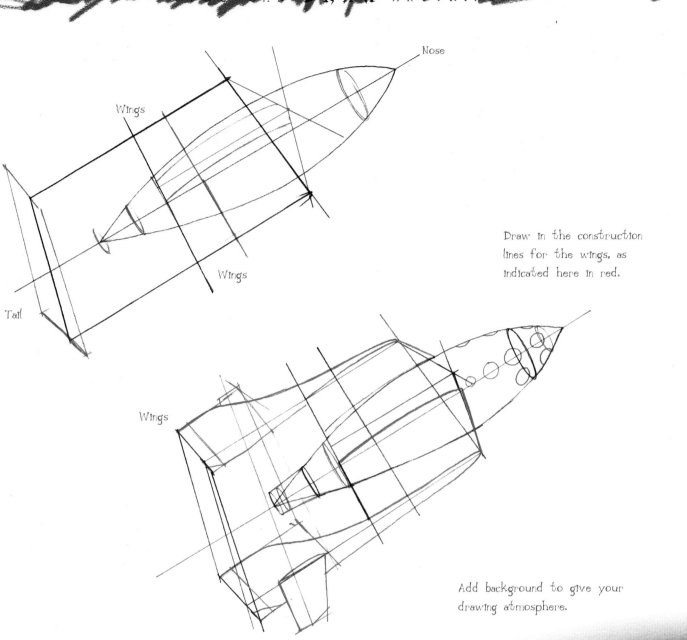

Nose

Wings

Wings

Tail

Draw in the construction
lines for the wings, as
indicated here in red.

Wings

Wings

Add background to give your
drawing atmosphere.

The engine of Space Ship One
has combined elements from
both solid and liquid rocket
motors. This is a unique engine
capable of accelerating to twice
the speed of sound.

When your drawing is
complete, remove construction
lines with an eraser.

Glossary

Chiaroscuro The use of light and dark shades in a drawing or painting.

Composition The position of a picture on the drawing paper.

Construction lines Structural lines used in the early stages of a drawing.

Fixative A type of resin used to spray over a finished drawing to prevent smudging* (see page 2).

Focal point A central point of interest.

Light source The direction the light is coming from.

Proportion The correct relationship of scale between parts of a drawing.

Reference Photographs or other images that can be drawn, if drawing from life is not possible.

Squaring up To transfer a drawing or photo accurately using square grids.

Three-dimensional An image that has the effect of making it look lifelike or real.

Index